HEART RHYTHMS 'N RHYMES

Trees

R O D   K R I E W A L L

WESTBOW
PRESS®
A DIVISION OF THOMAS NELSON
& ZONDERVAN

WestBow Press books may be ordered through booksellers or by contacting:

WestBow Press
A Division of Thomas Nelson & Zondervan
1663 Liberty Drive
Bloomington, IN 47403
www.westbowpress.com
1 (866) 928-1240

ISBN: 978-1-5127-1768-6 (sc)
ISBN: 978-1-5127-1769-3 (e)

Library of Congress Control Number: 2015917657

Print information available on the last page.

WestBow Press rev. date: 11/19/2015

To the women in my life. To my wife and two daughters, each of whom have encouraged me in all my writing, and especially to our daughter Faith, from whom the subject was requested and took root. And to our granddaughter, who, as she grows, I expect will likewise learn the joy of the climb.

CONTENTS

The Climb 1

Frame It 3

The Quilt 5

Embers 7

Ten Thousand Leaves 9

The Tree House 11

The Monument 13

The Garden 15

The Boxer 19

The Small One 21

Iamatree 23

Lemons 27

Arborist 29

The Stand 31

Returning 33

My Tree and I 35

The Park 37

The Walk 39

The Pile 41

Fruit or Nut 43

Pining 45

The Picnic 47

About the Author 49

THE CLIMB

From lofty bough with branch and twig
To buried roots, both small and big,
And hardy trunk with bark all 'round
That ties together the up and down.

The form's the same, and yet it's new.
Look again, and you'll see so too.
And whether seen in forests great
Or at a bus stop while you wait,

There is a majesty one can see—
The simple majesty of the tree.

Caught in backgrounds that one might miss
Or in a mind's eye reminisce
They're oft not center stage at all
But raise our gaze by standing tall.

Artists paint them in a scene alone
Or beside a river with sun-splashed stone.
Whether bare or green or of brilliant hue,
To each season they'll return anew.

And though by sight is the common choice,
We miss a lot if we miss their voice.

They'll whisper memories of years gone by.
They'll hum a song to sun and sky.
Or they'll call you to their shade below,
A protected respite from the world you know.

They laugh along with birds that peep.
They hush the world while nestlings sleep.
They rage right back against the storm.
They'll offer themselves to keep you warm.

So join me now within the tree.
I invite you to …come climb with me.

FRAME IT

Whether black-and-white or colored hue,
Whether child's paper or gallery queue,
Whether pencil sketch or photo's matte,
Whether 3-D logo or silhouette,
Whether from above or from below,
Whether sweltering heat or freezing snow,
Whether arid land or waterborne,
Whether forest wide or mount forlorn,
Whether life abundant, as in a zoo,
Whether life holding on, as a branch or two.

Still, in all, it pictures life.
It pictures strength overcoming strife.
It pictures winters that give rise to spring.
It pictures growth beyond suffering.
It pictures rest amidst glaring day.
It pictures fruitfulness along the way.
It pictures depth, both secure and firm.
It pictures shelter to which others turn.
It pictures big, which from small has grown.
It pictures years beyond our own.

So when it's seen with heart and thought
    Beyond the scene that eyes first sought,
The frame must be big to frame all you see
    When you really want to frame a tree.

THE QUILT

The living canopy after green has fled,
Now patchwork swatches, orange, yellow, red.
Seen from afar or overhead,
The quilt again laid on God's canopy bed.

 EMBERS

Dancing coals up in the sky,
Palm tree fronds on the wind's last sigh.
Burning embers going to and fro,
Edges ablaze by the sunset's glow.

TEN THOUSAND LEAVES

Ten thousand leaves waving, all saying hi,
    All waving still after you go by.
Ten thousand leaves basking, soaking the sun,
    Giving you shade for daytime fun.
Ten thousand leaves working, making new air,
    Doing their job, not caring if you care.
Ten thousand leaves fluttering, wrestling the breeze,
    Holding on tight even if you sit at ease.
Ten thousand leaves turning, as if autumn's their friend,
    Returning to soil, doing you good to the end.
So complain not at leaves, for they complain not at you.
    Smile back at them as they're waving to you,
    And know each tall tree has this by the score,
    For take ten thousand times twenty,
    And know if you wave,
    They wave more!

THE TREE HOUSE

Inward, upward, your eyes drawn in,
Shaded motions catch your eyes within.
Life is there within a nest,
A mother's weavings at their best.
Fleeting squirrels from branch to branch
Chase each other at the chance
To steal a nut or change their place,
Under leafy branch they jump and race.
Chattering flock on shaded limb,
A chorus form, a most raucous din.
Upon the trunk some peck for food,
While those below use roots as good
Shelter under their dark canopy,
Where food is found without need to see.
A busy place from edge to core,
The tree house full with room for more.

THE MONUMENT

Lifeless now alone it stands
A monument to forgotten lands—
Forgotten lands, forgotten times,
Forgotten tales, forgotten rhymes.

Forgotten but not lost it seems,
For life around it swarms and teems,
Teems with happenings of the day,
Even with no recall of yesterday.

Yesterday or yesteryear, not a thought, not a tear,
Not a memory, not a fear.

And so it stands amidst this life
A testament of unbidden strife—
Strife that came, no warning given,
Strife unwanted down from heaven.

All was peace, and then was not,
A flash fast gone that still burned hot,
Hot enough to take a life,
Smoldering ruins from a long, hot knife.

Long, hot knife piercing cloud and sky,
Where only after came the rumbling cry.

But that was then, and this is now.
Life goes on, as they say, somehow,
And somehow life overcomes the strife,
Overcomes the heat, overcomes the knife.

Life wins out, for it was made that way,
The way night will lose to the light of day,
For light of day shows what night would hide—
Hide fear's end, hide that not all has died.

And where light reveals, monuments remain.
Where life once stood, it will return again.
Again life wins, whether planned or no.
The monument standing tells us so.

THE GARDEN

"I planted a garden," the Lord said to me.
"Come and I will show it to you,"
So we walked together to see this place,
Just talking in the morning dew.

We rounded a hill, and there it was—
Just a glance, but I knew I was home.
I looked at the Lord and then walked right in.
While He watched, I began to roam.

Flowers splayed colors, waterfalls gushed,
And grasses rustled bright in the sun.
For a while I would walk, and for a while I would stare.
And for a while I would simply run.

But the best of all these and what made this place please
Was that this bursting garden was a garden of trees.

The trees all stood tall, no two the same,
Many with great fruits ripe to sup,
Lithe branches draped down, strong limbs reached out wide,
And great pillars of green stood straight up.

Finally I spoke and asked for their names,
For I only knew each one as a tree.
He said they were mine, that He gave them to me,
And whatever I said, they would be.

So cedar and oak and cherry and pear
And olive and fig they became,
Apple and pine and so many more,
Until every tree had its own name.

But the joy and the fun, between both shade and bright sun,
Changed when the Lord said to me, "We're not done."

Two trees remained, in the center of all,
       That I had not seen, but I needed to know.
I couldn't say why, but the way it was said
       Almost seemed as if reluctantly so.

So slower of pace but not overlong,
       Before the two trees we soon came.
Fruit they both had, but before I dared speak,
       He said that these two He must name.

The Tree of Life, He pointed out.
       As to its name, He did not tell me why—
The Tree of Knowledge of Good and Evil—
       He said the day I ate that fruit, I would die…

And you know the rest; with my helpmeet, though blessed,
I ate the wrong fruit and failed both the Lord and the test.

Though the garden remained, we had to leave,
       The angel now guarding us from the other tree,
But don't point at me and the choice that I made,
       For the same choice is now yours as you'll see.

The Tree of Life is not just for then;
       It's every choice that we pick what He's shown.
The Tree of Knowledge of Good and Evil
       Is any choice that we pick on our own.

It's the choice of our hearts; it's not really the tree.
      Will we trust God or want our own way?
So choose carefully each time which fruit will you pick,
      For that fruit you will eat in that day.

And as the saying goes, we are what we eat,
      And it fits here even more than we know,
For the fruit takes root, and we become the tree.
      What we become is what the Lord's trying to show.

We, like the tree, have fruit that we bear,
      Which can give life or last only that day.
And beyond all this there's still so much more
      As we continue along our way,

For each choice is a tree, and our life is a tree,
      And a tree comes from each fruit that we bear
Until a lifetime full makes a garden of trees,
      Which we name because we've put them there.

      "I am planting a garden," the Lord says again.
      "Come with me into what is yet to be.
There is fruit and flower and water and sun,
      And your choice of what trees you will see."

He will be like a tree firmly planted by streams of water,
Which yields its fruit in its season
And its leaf does not wither;
And in whatever he does, he prospers.

                                        —Psalm 1:3

17

 # THE BOXER

He bobs and weaves. His limbs reach long, towering over everything near.
This season's bouts will start anew, new foes to fight but not to fear.

Trunks are worn. There's added girth—another year seen in the ring.
He's getting old, but the strength's still there, though scars mark past suffering.

Lightning jabs have left their mark. There've been cuts and scrapes and burns,
But his friends still flock, and he holds them all up. And that's okay because he's learned

That sappy is good if you're made of wood,
   And to be the last one standing is the goal of a tree.

THE SMALL ONE

Not so tall, not so grand, not so breathtakingly fine,
Not the one others seek out, just rooted in its own place and time.

True to form, true to type, true to what it is,
Not drawing attention to itself, but that's okay; it's what it is.

For there are many more of the average or small than there are of the great and grand,
And a forest is made up of usual trees, and it's they that cover the land.

They still make you look up, and will last through the years and, once seen, will await your return.
Or to those who come after, they anew give their gift, of helping them grow and learn.

But know whether thicket or forest or grove, or clump or stand or wood,
Or shelter or growth or copse or brake,
      To the small one, they're all jungles and wildwood.

IAMATREE

All is dark, no room to move,
Still earth below, as like above,
Dry and dark and tightly cramped,
As if God Himself the ground had stamped.

How long, how deep, I do not know,
My memories hint that t'was not always so,
I think, I feel, that once was much more,
There was space above and light galore,
And moving things, and wind and sound,
And twisting, tossing up and down.

Why it changed or where it's gone,
If it indeed was real all along,
But for my part, I can't explain.
        From where do I remember rain?
And still I wait, here where I'm bound.
Is there freedom from this cold, hard ground?

The noise, the rumbling, lasts quite long,
But it plays a melody as a song,
Warming ground and softening earth,
Singing time to bring new life to birth.

Stretching now, I can finally move.
My case has cracked. I begin to shove.
One touch at first, it's moving slow,
But still I stretch and reach below.

A new hunger within me grows;
I need food, and food now to me flows.
I reach up, and can only trust,
For I'm on the move and grow I must.

Still stretching, reaching, both down and up,
I feel split in two but will not stop.
At last, at last, I at last break through
And start to glimpse a world I knew.

Warmth of sun and blue of sky,
They call me to raise myself on high
Yet more willingly now to the ground I cleave,
I from this soil now dare not leave.

For reaching down and farther out,
I find drinking, feasting all about.
Earth no longer is my tomb,
But my provision, my expanding room.

Now looking down from where I've come,
I feel secure how I've begun
To think again of what I once knew,
While holding earth, I reach t'ward blue.

But slowly, slowly it seems to go,
As grasses sprout fast and over me grow,
And still toward the sun I climb,
As a voice within says I'm on time.

It seems I've napped, the grass I knew,
Is gone and now is grown anew,
But I'm taller now. It stays beneath,
My growing count of branch and leaf.

Each nap repeats. I awake again,
Bigger stronger than what I'd been
The world around me shrinks as well,
Now birds and animals within me dwell.

From lofty heights I look around
At that which dwells around my ground.
I soak the sun, I dare the wind,
I drink the rain, and still stretch each limb.

And as I cast each timely seed,
How do I tell them what they need?
Do not be anxious when the ground is dark,
It's to hold you tight until new life can start.

LEMONS

Lemon, lemon on a tree,
Why can't you be more sweet for me?
Sour, sour in every slice
When being sweet would be so nice.

Lemon, lemon squeezed for me
With some water, now I see.
Add some sugar with a little care,
Pure refreshment made to share.

Dilute the tart and add the sweet,
And others will ask you for the treat.

Like a lemon on a tree,
Sometimes less than sweet are we,
Sour from work or our life pace,
But sour shared makes a sour face.

Dilute the tart and add the sweet,
Friends you'll make as friends you greet.

Lemon, lemon on a tree,
Why can't you be more sweet … like me?

ARBORIST

Arborist, naturist, hugger of a tree,
These are titles but not for me.
Climber, higher, or out on a limb,
These are descriptions of where I've been.

THE STAND

Shorn of limb and bark and root.
A dead thing now that all forsook.
Stripped of all to its very core,
You cannot recognize it anymore.

Pierced and raised and cross-limb fixed,
It holds the world entire transfixed.
Above the world and beneath the sky,
Its life once offered had to die.

But purpose great it had for me.
Its purpose met on Calvary.

The Tree of Life in the garden shone
The Tree of Life at Revelation's throne.
But in between it had to be
Where life met death in victory.

Across the years it stands there still,
A solitary stand upon a hill.
So glance again at boughs raised high
And tips that point you to the sky.

The Tree of Life was laid bare for me.
For Christ was crucified upon a tree.

RETURNING

Above the grass, below the leaves,
Flying back and forth with ease.
Head leaned back, feet kicked high,
Higher with each pass gone by.

The rope still there and almost new,
The rope replaced before they grew.
Still holds the seat of weathered wood,
All notched and carved as an old seat should.

Still with a creak but a bit more sway,
The branch still holds again this day.
And as it was before, it is again,
      As boys now men … are boys again.

MY TREE AND I

Feel the wind like a gale
        blow right through both rope and rail.
Goad the wind to keep the pace
        at your back as you turn your face.
For to see the world of seven seas,
        One must not fear but cheer each breeze.
And to the top one must climb
        to the crow's nest atop the spline.
No more to look to the world below
        but to look ahead where eye can't go.
As the world awaits, each voyage new,
        the wind affirms the sights are true.
Oh the sights I see in my mind's eye
        In the adventures of my tree and I.

THE PARK

Arches, spires, ascending wood,
Worshipful places for those who would.
Sacred shade and crafted bark,
Lead the pilgrim through the wooded park.

Life in tree, both heart and limb,
Life to creatures that rest within,
A peaceful balance within, without,
Each hears the other in silent shout.

It's not man's work, this place serene.
Though planned by man, it's not man's mean.
This peace, this harmony, this joy unfurled
Is a glimpse of heaven as another world.

So as you return again back through this place
And leave behind the crowd, the pace,
Just know that as you look above,
This place ordained is from the God of love.

The peace is His; the life is too.
The words without speech He's speaking to you.

Arches, spires, ascending wood,
Worshipful places for those who would.
Sacred shade in whole or part,
Call the pilgrim here to hear God's heart.

THE WALK

Gossamer moss draped on leaves
    that the bright full moon lights up with ease.
        Silvery shadows as you pass below,
           this mystical version of the world you know.
              The trees, the trees, why do they glow?
          Whispered rustlings add a voice
       to your own heart murmuring at your choice
    To walk these woods all on your own
Now that you're almost full grown.

'Tis easier in the light of day
    to singly pass along this way.
        With the sun so bright and oh so warm,
           Why should one fear? There is no harm.
              The trees, the trees, no longer charm.
          But that has passed; the world has changed,
       and all soft edges are rearranged.
    Now it tilts, now it snags
Below blackening sky and towering crags.

Roots are reaching from their place
    to trip your feet's anxious hurried pace.
        The leaves brush by and feel like webs
           and fill your thoughts with things you dread.
              The trees, the trees are in your head.
          The moon itself has run to hide
       as jet-black clouds below it ride
    Upon the sky to watch this play
That has begun anew at end of day.

Which now knows fear as fear that grows
　　That watches all and all things knows.
　　　　The voice is choked the breathing fast,
　　　　　　As the future dims and joins the past.
　　　　　　　　The trees, the trees, their shadows cast.
　　　　　All light is gone. Gone is the way
　　　　That seemed so plain before in day.
　　The path begun is there no more.
The trees at dark have shown their core.

And then it's there, the beacon bright
　　That brings back hope out of the night.
　　　　The lighted sill, the open door
　　　　　　All call you back to life once more.
　　　　　　　　The trees, the trees, betray no more.
　　　　　The family greets and brings you in.
　　　　The world is safe as e'er has been.
　　The adventure done, no fear must show.
Was the mind deceived? Was it real or no?

The trees, the trees, what do they know?

40

THE PILE

Leaving the leaves under the tree
To make a big pile that we can see
Leaves the leaving from under the tree
Something for you but not for me
Until the leaves left under the tree
Are all left wishing … they were back up in the tree!

 # FRUIT OR NUT

"Fruit or Nut, sliced or cut,
how would you like it served?"

"I'll just take it straight, right on my plate,
just from the tree is preferred."

"That won't work for olives, and lemons are sort of
too sour to eat that way,

But I'll do as you wish and give you a dish
of whatever will make your day."

"I'll take one sample of each, maybe two of the peach,
and be sure to leave nothing out,

And when I am done, I'll be the happiest one
whom you have served here, without a doubt."

"I am very impressed. You sure did your best.
I thought your stomach would curl."

"But I am made for such stuff. Eating's not tough
when you're serving up food to a squirrel."

PINING

Their needles and cones, not so soft,
A bedding of choice do not make.
But comfort is not their purpose in life,
So what else from them would you take?

They are made to survive through cold and snow
And wind-driven ice and rain.
They thrive where it's harsh all on their own
To welcome the springtime again.

Constant are they, ever-clothed, evergreen,
Though they may sharp and pointed be,
In all seasons you'll find them the same;
In winter they're the Christmas tree.

So may you have friends as faithful as they,
Unchanging and to the point in their good.
And know the pricks you feel when you get close to them
Come from a heart of tender softwood.

THE PICNIC

The blanket on the lawn is laid,
Green and red and yellow plaid.
The tray upon the blanket sits.
The tea is steeped amidst the set.

The bees are buzzing above the blooms,
The birds all chirping their varied tunes.
While two girls chatting in the shade
Sip their tea with crackers and marmalade.

And in the background amidst it all,
The old apple tree is standing tall.
The scene below it has seen before,
Whether the prior year or a hundred more.

The days, the seasons, the generations change,
And time will often rearrange.
But the old tree offers more than apples sweet.
It offers a world in which kindred spirits meet.

ABOUT THE AUTHOR

Rod Kriewall has been writing creatively ever since high school where he took 3rd in a statewide writing competition. He grew up on a farm in the upper Midwest where he attended church and professed faith in Christ at an early age. His professional career led him to the Pacific island of Guam before settling in California. In addition to writing, he has spent much of his life studying and teaching the Bible and, along with his wife, being actively involved in Christian ministry. When asked to turn his creativity toward trees, the result shows not only the prominence and appreciation that trees have in God's creation, but also the love of climbing trees and the joy that growing up around, and in, trees, has been to his life.

Printed in the United States
By Bookmasters